R
99p

HORSES

First published in Great Britain 1984 by
Webb and Bower (Publishers) Limited
9 Colleton Crescent, Exeter, Devon EX2 4BY

Edited, designed and illustrated by
the E.T. Archive Limited
Chelsea Wharf, 15 Lots Road, London SW10 0QH

Designed by Julian Holland
Picture Research by Anne-Marie Ehrlich
Special photography by Eileen Tweedy
Copyright © text and illustrations E.T. Archive Ltd 1984

British Library Cataloguing in Publication Data

Seth-Smith, Michael
   Horses.—(A Webb & Bower miniature)
   1. Horses—Pictorial works
   I. Title
   636.1'0022'2   SF303

   ISBN 0–86350–016–1

Phototypeset by Text Filmsetters Limited, Orpington, Kent
Printed and bound in Hong Kong by Mandarin Offset International Limited

HORSES

Michael Seth-Smith

Webb & Bower

EXETER, ENGLAND

Horses of Ancient Greece

Homer referred to war chariots drawn by two small horses almost 3000 years ago, and Herodotus, born in 484 BC, claimed that the Greeks learned much from the Libyans about the breeding of horses. His claim must be respected for he spent several years touring north Africa and wrote that his fellow countrymen had been taught by Libyans how to yoke four horses together. Most information about the horses of ancient Greece comes from the works of Xenophon (430-359 BC), an Athenian cavalry commander, who stressed the need to take care of the feet of horses and offered suggestions for methods to harden them. Horseshoes, saddles and stirrups were unknown in this era.

Chariots were necessary in battle because small-sized horses and ponies were unable to carry an armed soldier for more than a short distance. The Greeks loved chariot races, and concentrated on breeding horses with suitable speed to win such contests, especially those at the Olympic Games, an event held every four years. Originally these races were for chariots pulled by four horses but by 408 BC two-horse chariot races were instituted.

The grey or white horses of Thessaly, a vast fertile plain, were probably the best breed in Greece where the mountainous country and small plains proved unsuitable for the breeding and rearing of stock on a large scale. Bucephalus, Alexander the Great's charger, was reputedly Thessalian bred.

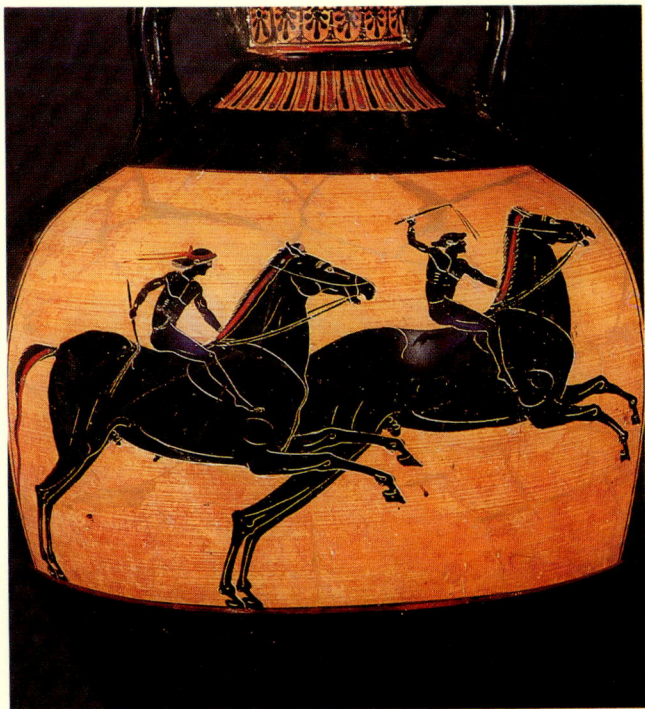

Horses of Ancient China

There was little interest in the breeding of horses in China until the opening of trade routes to the West in about 200 BC. Stimulated by travellers' tales of magnificent steeds of far greater quality than the humble ponies that they possessed, the Chinese realized that invasions by mounted horsemen could best be repelled with their own horsemen and they acquired horses by wholesale theft, tribute payments and as peace settlements from their vanquished enemies. Some of these horses, known as 'heavenly horses' by the Chinese, came from northern Afghanistan, where a local king had unwisely come to blows with Emperor Wu-ti. The Emperor's armies returned to China with several thousand horses of better quality than his own, and he deliberately set about improving the breed of his equine population. Many of his Mongolian ponies had lived in herds in the semi-desert and on the bleak steppes where any form of fodder was scarce, and where the temperature could vary from extreme cold to intense heat.

During the Eastern Han Dynasty (202 BC–AD 221) the authority and influence of a state was often measured by the number of chariots that it possessed while the rank of an official would be judged by the number of carriages he owned. For the most part only the rich and powerful had the use of chariots, but they also acquired horses and ponies for hunting and hawking, and for playing a game which was similar to polo.

Genghis Khan and Tamerlane

Genghis Khan, son of a powerful Mongol overlord who ruled a region to the west of the Great Wall of China, was born in AD 1162. Fifty years later, as titular head of many hundreds of tribes, he raised an army which included thousands of horsemen and invaded China. After three years of war he captured Peking before turning his attention to the west, attacking Persia, Afghanistan and the Caucasus. When he died in 1227, his empire stretched from Persia to China, but it gradually disintegrated through civil war and feud.

Towards the end of the fourteenth century, a new great leader appeared on the scene. Tamerlane (or Timur the Lame) was born in about 1336 in Transoxiana, a desolate and wild area north of Afghanistan. Gaining control of province after province, his power became absolute and he was hailed as overlord of a vast empire. In 1402 he defeated the Ottomans and acquired Asia Minor as his prize. Before his death in 1405, his influence was as strong as that of Alexander the Great and Genghis Khan. There is little evidence as to the breed of horses that he employed although it is accepted that his followers had horses of Arab strains, possibly the ancestors of the Akhal-Teké, in addition to their Mongolian ponies. When one of these ponies with a fine record of achievement died, its rider would pluck hairs from its tail and mane, string a musical instrument with them and tour his land singing praises to the dead pony.

The Trojan Horse

One of the most famous horses in history was made from wood. The plan behind its creation was most ingenious and succeeded totally. The Greek armies under Agamemnon, King of Mycenae, had laid unsuccessful siege to the city of Troy for more than ten years. Eventually Odysseus devised a scheme which although unorthodox, would enable them to capture the city.

A huge wooden horse was built and Greek soldiers (reputedly about thirty) hid in its belly. The remainder of the armies sailed away to trick the Trojans into believing that they had conceded defeat. The wooden horse, to which wheels had been fitted so that it could be dragged without difficulty, intrigued the Trojans. At nightfall, encouraged by Sinon – a relative of Odysseus, who pretended desertion and promised the safety of Troy from future Greek attack if the horse was brought to the temple of Athene – they hauled the horse into the centre of Troy and celebrated the departure of the Greeks, disregarding a warning from Laocoön, the priest of Apollo, 'I fear the Greeks, especially when they bring gifts'. By early morning the majority of the Trojans were in a drunken stupor. At a signal from Sinon, the Greeks climbed through a trapdoor concealed in the horse, and quickly opened the gates to their returning armies. The Trojans were slaughtered and the city fell to the triumphant Greeks.

St George

In the Middle Ages dragons symbolized sin. They were frequently depicted by painters as winged crocodiles with the tail of a serpent, while in medieval literature they were characterized as the evil custodians of captive maidens. It is understandable, therefore, that St George should be portrayed as the slayer of these monsters, for he was considered a valiant man and the epitome of chivalry. No precise details exist as to his career, but it has been claimed that he was martyred at Lydda in AD 303 for boldly criticizing the religious persecution of Christians by the Emperor Diocletian. Another claim is that he was little more than a soldier of fortune who was murdered in Alexandria before his mutilated body was thrown into the sea.

Whether these claims are true or false his name was mentioned by Richard Coeur de Lion who claimed that he had seen a vision of St George promising his victory over the Saracens. At the Council of Oxford in 1222 it was decreed that the feast day of St George, 23 April, should be a national festival.

A legendary hero, his emblem of a red cross on a white background became widely recognized, his standard was proudly carried by English monarchs on their campaigns, and his name became the battle cry of English soldiers. He was made patron saint of England by Edward III.

ST GEORGE AND THE DRAGON.

Knights in Armour

The word 'knight' is derived from the Saxon 'kneht' mean-
ing a man-at-arms or a servant to the king. In medieval
days, the knight would have been a man of gentle birth who
in his youth had served as a page at court or as an attendant
in the retinue of a nobleman, before being admitted with
due ceremony to a degree of military rank and awarded the
right to bear arms. William Shakespeare made reference to
the chivalry shown by knights,

> Knights by their oaths, should right poor ladies harms,

and commented upon the honour which could be bestowed
upon a soldier for acts of gallantry,

> A soldier by the honour-giving hand of Coeur-de-Lion,
>   knighted in the field.

In battle, the heavily-armoured knight was unable to play
an important role until the introduction of stirrups, for
without them he could not retain his balance in the saddle
whilst wielding a lance, spear, sword or battleaxe. His
armour would weigh as much as 40 lb (18 kg), and under his
shirt of mail, made of small interwoven steel rings, he
would wear garments of leather. Over his breastplate he
wore a coloured blouse emblazoned with his coat of arms.

Triumvirate of Stallions

The modern Thoroughbred traces his ancestry to three famous Arabian stallions. The first to arrive in England was the Byerley Turk, acquired by Captain Robert Byerley from a Turkish officer during fighting in Hungary. Byerley, who commanded the 6th Dragoon Guards, rode his charger at the Battle of the Boyne. The stallion was sent to stud at Middridge Hall in County Durham and later stood at Goldsborough Hall near York, where he founded a dynasty which can be followed through to such twentieth-century heroes as The Tetrarch, Tourbillon and Blakeney.

In 1704 Mr Thomas Darley, English Consul in Aleppo, bought a stallion from Sheik Mirza for 300 sovereigns. Known as the Darley Arabian, he stood 14.2 hands and was considered faultless in symmetry. He took up duties as a stallion at Aldby Park, the Darley estate in East Yorkshire where he remained until 1730. The modern lines of St Simon, Gainsborough and Blandford who sired four Derby winners can be traced back to him.

The third stallion was the Godolphin Arabian, foaled in the Yemen in 1724. Exported to Tunis he was given by the Bey to Louis XIV before being bought by Edward Coke of Longford Hall in Derbyshire. On Coke's death the stallion became the property of the Earl of Godolphin who sent him to his Gog Magog stud near Newmarket. The contemporary blood-lines of Hurry On and Precipitation are related to the Godolphin Arabian who died at the age of twenty-nine.

The Thoroughbred

Throughbreds have been described as 'the aristocrats of the horse world' for they have no equal for speed, stamina, courage and conformation. They must be registered in the General Stud Book which was first published almost 200 years ago. The compiler of the original GSB, James Weatherby, set out in alphabetical order a list of every mare of whom he had information, and appended details of all their progeny, giving the year of birth, colour, sex, sire and wherever possible the name. This system proved so satisfactory that it been maintained with only a few modifications to the present day.

One of the first Thoroughbreds to gain immortality was Eclipse who was born on 1 April 1764. A small chestnut colt bred by the Duke of Cumberland, he was never beaten on the racecourse and was 'allowed by all ranks to be the fleetest horse that ever ran in England'. He won eighteen races before being retired to stud at Clay Hill near Epsom. He sired three Derby winners and has influenced the evolution of the modern Thoroughbred through his sons King Fergus, and Pot-8-os, who received his astonishing name from an illiterate stableboy, who when told to paint the name 'Potatoes' on the horse's box spelt it Pot-oooooooo! Today the champion Thoroughbred has precocity, speed and the ability to race over far shorter distances than his ancestors, many of whom did not see a racecourse until they were five-year-olds.

Polo

A form of polo was played in Persia and Afghanistan more than 700 years ago, with initiative, horsemanship and dare-devilry needed by riders wishing to master the game. The British in India took up polo after the Mutiny had been crushed, and it soon became as popular with the regiments stationed on the North West Frontier as tennis and hockey had been in the past. Ponies, many of them imported from Australia as remounts for the Indian cavalry were cheap, and it was quickly realized that polo was one of the fastest and most exciting ball games. The game obsessed many young officers, particularly those of the 9th Lancers and 10th Hussars who demonstrated an eight-a-side game of polo at Hounslow Heath in England in 1874. Soon polo was played at Ranelagh, Roehampton and Hurlingham and rules were laid down by the Hurlingham Club. Initially the size of a polo pony was limited, but this restriction was lifted at the end of World War I.

Polo was also played in the USA and Argentina. The Westchester Cup became the most prized polo trophy in the USA, and although won by an English team in 1882, 1900 and 1902 the Americans dominated the Cup in the next two decades. The Argentinians, however, were breeding the almost perfect polo pony which showed the speed and the character of a Thoroughbred allied to the toughness of the Spanish Creole breed. These ponies were later supplied as foundation stock to both the American and English polo teams.

Foxhunting

In rural England the stag and the hare had been hunted in forest and woodland for centuries on slow sturdy horses. With the disappearance of the forests, sportsmen discovered the thrill of hunting the fox which they had previously been accustomed merely to digging out. They also discovered that foxhunting was far more exhilarating, for fences, including dangerous bullfinch and double oxer, had to be jumped at speed in order to keep up with hounds running fast over open country. Gradually a new breed of horse emerged which had the desired speed combined with the stamina to carry the rider for long periods over the toughest country. By the mid-eighteenth century, the pioneers of modern foxhunting were making their appearance, headed by Hugo Meynell in the 'Shires'. He was the first Master to look for speed in his hounds, and was also one of the first to believe that preparation for the chase consisted of 'a good blazing fire at 6 a.m., a splendid buttock of beef, or a venison pasty, with chocolate and a jug of old October'. During the Peninsular War the Duke of Wellington kept a pack of hounds behind Torres Vedras as he believed that foxhunting was a fine test of courage for his officers, and later Robert Surtees, creator of the lovable Mr Jorrocks, wrote that foxhunting was 'the image of war without the guilt'. It was feared that the advent of the railways would ruin 'Hunting England' but the fears were groundless as were worries that two world wars would end it.

Dressage

The ancient Greeks were the first equestrians to be intrigued and fascinated by dressage – the training of horses. By the sixteenth century the skill demanded by advanced dressage received new impetus when Federico Grisone founded a riding academy in Naples, and subsequently published a book on equitation which was acclaimed throughout Europe. Riding academies mushroomed as equestrian education became popular and a necessary part of a young aristocrat's life.

In England, William Cavendish, Duke of Newcastle (1592-1676) was renowned for his horsemanship and his knowledge of the performance of dressage. A devoted royalist, he fought gallantly for Charles I, virtually bankrupting himself in the process, until he was compelled to flee to Holland after the King's defeat at Marston Moor. In Antwerp he established a riding school and wrote *New Methods of Dressing the Horse* which became a landmark in the development of equestrianism. Less than a century later, François Robichon, Sieur de la Guerinière, one of the world's greatest exponents of horsemanship, highlighted the art of dressage and the principles of equitation, and insisted that his aim was to make horses supple, loose, flexible, compliant and obedient.

The Director of the Spanish Riding School declared recently that, 'the dressage rider is an artist, and the horse his medium; together they produce a work of art'.

Passades au Petit Galop,
la demy-volte a Main Gauche.

Passades a toute Bride, la demy-
volte à Main Gauche.

25

Steeplechasing

Steeplechasing originated in Ireland in the mid-eighteenth century. Reckless horsemen would dare others of equal impetuosity to follow them across country intersected with high banks, stone walls and wide ditches. The leader would choose as dangerous a course as possible, often taking a church steeple as a landmark for his line of direction. Gradually the name 'steeplechasing' was given to these contests, but they did not find favour in England until the hunting men of Leicestershire decided to follow the example of the Irish gentry. The first recorded steeplechase in which there were more than two starters was in 1792 when Mr Charles Meynell won a race over an eight-mile course from Barkby Holt to Billesden Coplow. It is not true to claim the first steeplechase in England was 'The Midnight Steeplechase' in which a number of soldiers in blue overalls, nightshirts and conical shaped night-caps, were said to have raced from their barracks near Ipswich to Nacton Church, for the event was solely in the imagination of the artist, Henry Alken. He always regretted his error in failing to have the silhouette of the gate shattered.

In the 1920s and early 30s, steeplechasing was known as being 'only for the needy and greedy' but today it is more highly regarded due to the exploits of such renowned horses as Golden Miller, Arkle and Red Rum.

Circus Horses

Londoners first saw a circus when Philip Astley and his wife gave exhibitions of trick-riding in a field near Lambeth in the 1760s. Astley had been a soldier in the Light Dragoons and on his discharge as a sergeant-major had been given a white stallion by his commanding officer. This horse and another which Astley had bought, amazed and entertained Londoners with the tricks that they performed when ridden by their master. Astley realized that it was easier to retain his balance on a cantering horse if it travelled in a circle. In doing this, he traced the first ring.

The three principal types of circus horse are Ring horses, Liberty horses and Haute Ecole horses. Ring horses must have a tolerant and placid disposition in addition to wide backs because the clowns deliberately pretend to annoy them while they are being ridden around the ring-side. The Haute Ecole horses perform intricate dressage manoeuvres whereas the Liberty horses usually work in teams under the conductorship of their trainer. When it is first put into training, the Liberty horse is exercised on a lunging rein with a rider on its back. As it becomes accustomed to his trainer's commands and understands the signficance of the pressure on the reins, it learns to follow instructions made by the trainer's whip. The rider gradually takes less part and eventually the horse performs riderless.

The Horse in Agriculture

The horse has long been a vital feature in agriculture and its 'maid of all work' dominance ended only with the coming of the motorized tractor and other modern equipment. More useful than the ox or the mule, the horse was, by the twelfth century, recognized throughout northern Europe as an invaluable asset to all farmers. One drawback, however, was that the horse cost more to feed than the ox or mule, requiring expensive corn rather than grass.

It was customary for mares to be used in ploughing, with those bred in Flanders especially favoured because they worked hard continually from dawn until dusk. Gradually, breeds of heavy horses evolved whose powers of endurance were outstanding. In East Anglia, farmers boasted that their Suffolk Punch could plough more land in a day than any other breed. In Leicestershire, Staffordshire and Derbyshire Shire horses played a significant part as farm and draught horses, and as land cultivation became more sophisticated, their importance steadily increased.

Many painters have found inspiration in the world of agriculture, including George Morland (1763-1804) and John Constable (1776-1837). Constable's *Flatford Mill* expresses his love of the Suffolk countryside and respect for farmers, many of whom he counted among his friends.

Heavy Horses of Britain

Two of the recognized breeds of heavy horses in Britain are the Suffolk Punch and the Shire. The pure bred Suffolk Punch which has earned a nation-wide reputation, is usually chestnut in colour, more agile than any other breeds of heavy horse, and has immense girth, powerful hindquarters and stands on short legs. These short legs make it seem top heavy, but do not affect its strength which is amply demonstrated at 'pulling' matches. Over the years, it has been successfully developed as a farm horse. Its ancestry has been traced back to a horse foaled in 1760, but may date back even further to the Viking invasions.

The Shire is believed to be descended from the medieval horse known as the 'Great Horse' or 'English Black'. It has been described as having 'size, weight, strength and docility' but has lacked speed. Nevertheless its future seems assured, for a few dedicated breeders and a number of commercial firms continue to use Shire horses for short haul purposes. Britain's brewers have always been renowned for their Shire horses which remain on farms for the first five years of their life, being taught to wear heavy harness and to draw a cart. One of the hardest training tasks is to teach the prospective dray-horse to back while in the shafts, but it is essential, for on many occasions it must manoeuvre a heavily laden dray in crowded streets.

The Blacksmith

Blacksmiths were acknowledged to be among the finest craftsmen in England during the Middle Ages, and were greatly respected in villages throughout the land. In addition to making axes and ploughs in his forge where the hearth was heated by charcoal, the blacksmith was also expected to repair all iron farm implements.

The patron saint of blacksmiths is St Dunstan who was also Archbishop of Canterbury. Legend claims that he pinched the Devil by the nose with a pair of tongs when the forces of evil in the form of a beautiful maiden tried to tempt him. The pinching was made the more horrific because the tongs were red hot. Only then did the Devil realize that the Archbishop was a blacksmith as well as a saint.

Once it became necessary for horses to be shod as a result of improved road surfaces, the blacksmith's trade took on an extra dimension. It is thought that a rudimentary horseshoe was first used by ancient Britons to protect the horse's feet on roads built by the Roman conquerors. Modifications were made later, and the adage, 'no foot, no horse', proved to be correct on many occasions. Fullering – making a groove on the underside of the shoe to increase the grip, evolved in the sixteenth century, and clips, to keep the shoe in place, more than two hundred years later.

Stagecoaches

Few people travelled further than absolutely necessary until the early seventeenth century. The roads were atrocious, the threat of being robbed ever present, and the journeying time out of all proportion to the distance involved, particularly in winter. It was not surprising, therefore, that villagers would welcome the first coach each spring by offering the passengers and the coachmen bread, cakes and wine to celebrate the end of winter.

The first coaches had been built in Hungary in the early sixteenth century but in England it was another fifty years before Walter Rippon built a coach for the Earl of Rutland.

After the Civil War, coaches linked London with the bigger cities, but a ten-mile journey could still take six hours because of the poor roads. Improvement was slow although eventually some three thousand coaches networked England, with the fastest of them reaching ten miles an hour. 'Nimrod' was to comment, 'Coach travelling is no longer a disgusting and tedious labour, but has long since been converted into comparative ease and really approaches something like luxury'. Yet cruelty to horses had not abated. The coachmen, meagrely paid and often tipped by travellers grateful for the punctual arrival of their coach, would flog their horses, occasionally using a cat-o'-nine tails whip known as 'The Apprentice'. It was seldom that coach horses survived for more than six years under such treatment.

Mail Coaches

The enterprising John Palmer planned a system of government-controlled Royal Mail coaches to replace the existing carriage of mail on horseback. He received support eventually from William Pitt, then Chancellor of the Exchequer. The first mail coach left Bristol for London at 4 p.m. on 2 August 1784 and arrived at the General Post Office headquarters in London the following morning. These coaches provided a far more efficient and exclusive service than that offered by the stagecoaches, for each one carried a guard armed with a blunderbuss, pistols and a horn which was blown to announce the arrival of the coach at various specified halts. It was the custom to paint the wheels red and the body maroon, with the royal arms in gold on the doors. The coaches took precedence over all others on the road, and were driven by teams of four which were changed at frequent intervals. The coachmen and the guards prided themselves upon the punctuality of the coaches.

By the early 1800's, coaches were better sprung and roads were becoming macadamized. A journey from London to South Yorkshire could be completed in less than one day compared to the four days it had previously taken. Thomas de Quincey described the nightly scene at the GPO, 'Horses. Can these be horses who bound off with action and gestures of leopards. What stir! What sea-like ferment. What a thunder of wheels, what a trampling of hoofs. What a sounding of trumpets. What farewell cheers.'

Shetland Ponies

It has been assumed that Shetland ponies were the first equines to be brought to Britain, having originated along the western coasts of France and Spain. Subsequently other ponies were brought to the Shetland and Orkney Islands by the Norwegians. Therefore the Shetland pony is probably a composite breed of a small western European animal and a Scandinavian animal. Certainly they served an invaluable purpose in the Islands once they became acclimatized to the bleak northern conditions – gale force winds and constant storms throughout the winter. Feed was always in scarce supply, and shelter against the elements almost non-existent.

As the centuries passed the Shetland pony evolved as a rugged-coated animal with a thick mane and tail as protection against the weather, and an equally tough and sturdy character. It was used as a pack and saddle pony to drag turf from the moors to the coastal villages, and to take seaweed from the shore inland to those farmers who used it as fertiliser. One Victorian visitor noticed that sometimes their forelegs were manacled together causing them to hobble like rabbits.

The Shetland first appeared in England in about 1770 and in later years many of them laboured in the coal-mines where their size, temperament and toughness made them indispensable for pulling heavy loads from the coal-face to the surface.

New Forest Ponies

Ponies have roamed the New Forest in the south of England for more than a thousand years. There is better shelter than in the Shetland Islands, and consequently the New Forest ponies do not possess the same rugged characteristics as their northern relations, although their constitution is strong and they can survive on poor grazing land. It is probable that all native pony breeds in Britain were originally derived from the same indigenous stock. Nevertheless the New Forest ponies, because there are so many ports and safe harbours on the south coast, may have more Arab strains in their make-up than other breeds of ponies in Britain. Some of these strains may even have been introduced by the Romans. In the nineteenth century, several local farmers attempted to improve the breed by introducing Arab strains once again, using stallions belonging to the Lord Warden of the New Forest, Prince Albert.

Within the next two decades, stallions of other native breeds including ponies from Exmoor, Dartmoor, Cumberland and Wales were introduced, and in 1910 a New Forest Pony Stud Book was published. To qualify for entry in subsequent editions, the pony's dam had to be a registered pony mare which had run in the New Forest for a minimum of a season as a three-year-old or upwards, and its sire had to be a pony stallion known by the Verderers of the Forest.

The Horse in War

The horse has assisted man in warfare since time immemorial. The ponies of the Scythians and Mongols helped them to subjugate their enemy on countless occasions. At Hastings in 1066 the cavalry won the day for William the Conqueror, although at Agincourt in 1415 the French horsemen proved no match for the English archers. Oliver Cromwell exploited his horsemen to great advantage in the battles of the Civil War in the 1640s, and may with justification be considered the pioneer of the correct use of cavalry. The ill-fated cavalry charge of the Light Brigade at Balaclava on 25 October 1854 was immortalized by Tennyson,

> When can their glory fade?
> O the wild charge they made!
> All the world wonder'd.
> Honour the charge they made
> Honour the Light Brigade
> Noble six hundred!

In November 1917 at the Battle of Cambrai tanks were used in numbers for the first time. In 1928 the 11th Hussars and the 12th Lancers were converted to armoured-car units. In World War II, however, Polish cavalry heroically charged German tanks, and the Russians employed more than thirty cavalry divisions. Although the King's Dragoon Guards were still using horses for mounted patrol work in 1943, the days of the horse in war were practically over.

The Horse in Art

Man's affection for the horse has been illustrated in Stone Age cave drawings, murals, paintings and sculpture. In England, equestrian art reached a peak in the days of Queen Anne, when Pieter Tillemans decided to earn his living as a painter at Newmarket, and has since then produced men of genius such as George Stubbs, Ben Marshall, John Ferneley and Sir Alfred Munnings. In the seventeenth and early eighteenth centuries, artists attempted to flatter the horses that they were commissioned to paint in order to please their patrons. Thus accuracy was frequently overlooked. George Stubbs, born in 1724, was more honest and had a good understanding of the anatomy of the horse whose qualities and defects he faithfully reproduced. Through the work of Stubbs and later painters, the evolution of the Thoroughbred is clearly shown, with the original Arab characteristics fined down, the horse's neck becoming narrower, his head larger, and his size increasing.

In the twentieth century, no English painter has displayed greater skill than Sir Alfred Munnings, the son of a Suffolk miller. Whether his paintings are showing racehorses at Newmarket, ponies on Exmoor, or Masters of the Foxhounds on their favourite hunters, his work has a vitality, freshness and sense of sunlight that few other artists have achieved.